Whether French is the
the fifth, you have prob
about the right and w
people say French is dif.... .. ..; others say it's easy.
Some consider grammar to be the most important aspect
of a language while others prefer to avoid it for as long as
possible.

Unless you are an experienced language learner, you
probably have a hard time figuring out who is right and
who is wrong. You probably don't know where to start
and may even fear that you will never be able to speak
French fluently. We all have these fears that are the result
of years spent studying languages the wrong way.

After years spent studying English and German at the
University, learning Korean on my own, helping people
like you learn French, and researching the best ways to
learn a new language, I have found a fun and effective way
to learn languages.

I wrote this book to help you discover the tools and
methods that I, and many language learners around the
world, use to learn languages. These are tools and methods
you can easily implement, to not only make learning
French easier, but also much more fun. And you want to
know the best thing about these methods? Most of them
won't cost you a dime.

Please note that this is not a textbook. You won't learn
French with this book. What you will learn is different
ways to learn French that are both fun and effective. After

reading this book, you will have all the knowledge and tools you need to finally become fluent in French.

Ready? C'est parti !

Contents

PART ONE: The fundamentals of learning French

PART TWO Mastering the four core language skills

PART ONE
The fundamentals of learning French

Chapter One

The most common myths about French and languages in general

You need to be gifted to learn French

Talent is cheaper than table salt. What separates the talented individual from the successful one is a lot of hard work. Stephen King

Before you actually get started learning French, let's review the most common language learning myths. Some of these myths can considerably slow you down and keep you from learning French efficiently. In fact, these myths are the main reason so many people fail at learning French. Learning French is simply a matter of believing in yourself, and believing that you can succeed. You may not realize it, but your doubts can result in very real learning restrictions. If you think you are not talented enough to learn French, you will most likely never be fluent in French. The same goes for many other activities. If you go to Paris expecting people to be rude, you will find rude people; whereas, if you go with an open mind, you are likely to encounter friendly, helpful people. You cannot control everything, of course, but you can at least control your thoughts and actions, and make sure that you are mentally prepared for success and not for failure. You may have already experienced failure in learning French, but now you can choose to use proven and effective methods that will help you reach your goals.

Back in high school, I believed that people were either good or bad at learning languages, and that only a select few were good at learning languages. I also thought that polyglots were extremely gifted individuals who could learn languages effortlessly, and I was absolutely convinced that my inability to learn English was a sign that I wasn't meant to speak foreign languages.

At that time, I had been learning English and German for six years, and still couldn't say anything more than "Hello, I am fine, thank you, and you?" I felt terrible about my inability to learn after putting in so much effort for so many years. I knew people who spoke several languages fluently, and yet here I was, unable to master even one language other than my native language. Yet, deep inside, I knew that the lack of talent couldn't be the only reason of my failure. I didn't consider myself stupid, and teachers and friends had told me I was certainly smart, based on how well I did in other learning endeavors. So I always ended up asking myself why others could learn a new language and I could not.

That's when I started reading stories from people saying they had found a way to learn languages fast. Honestly, it sounded a bit spammy. I had been trying to learn English for years and these people were saying that I could learn a language in less than a year? Were they trying to sell me something? They were not selling anything and this is what convinced me to give it a try. ; I had nothing to lose, after all. In the worst case, I would just remain a monoglot forever. In the best case, I would finally understand English and be able to discover a new world. I was more motivated than I had ever been.

Six months later, I was fluent in English.

Did I suddenly become more talented? Did I discover a secret pill allowing me to learn anything in a short time and without effort? Nope. Instead, two things happened. First, since I was more motivated, I started studying more regularly. Second, I started using methods like SRS, mnemonics (you will learn more about that in the chapter "How To Learn Vocabulary And Never Forget It") and decided to do what I had always been terrified of doing: practice English.

After successfully learning English, I decided to learn German, and later, Korean. This time, I used the techniques and tools I had discovered, which allowed me to reach a good level in Korean after just two months. Considering Korean was much harder to learn (as a native French speaker) than English, I was proud of myself. I wasn't fluent, but I could have a basic conversation and it was enough for my daily life in Korea. Most importantly, for the first time in my life, I was having fun learning a language. If you struggle to learn French, you should know there is nothing wrong with you. You may simply not be using the right method and tools.

Successful language learners spend countless hours learning languages, acquiring vocabulary and practicing speaking. There is no such thing as a "gift for languages".." There are simply people who follow effective methods and people who do not know the most effective methods for them.

Sure, you could argue that some people have a higher IQ, that it helps them learn languages. And you would be right, but to what extent? If you read the biographies of successful people, you will see that most of them didn't succeed because of their incredible intelligence,; they succeeded because they did their best and never gave up. In fact, many people fail every day, not because of low IQ, but because they don't use the right methods or don't work long enough or hard enough. One thing you can be sure of is that anyone, at any age, can learn French. If you work hard and implement effective learning strategies, you will learn French much faster and much better than you ever thought possible.

The Irish polyglot Benny Lewis, famous for learning a new language every three months, confessed that he didn't know any language other than English at age 21. He even had difficulties speaking English at first and needed speech therapy as a kid. It was only years later, after discovering that learning languages is not as hard as he thought, that he learned several languages and became the polyglot he is today.

And he is not alone. You can find thousands of similar stories on the internet.

It's easier to learn a language as a child

Another common language myth is the idea that children can learn languages more easily than adults. Numerous studies have proven that this is just a myth and that adult learners actually learn faster and more easily … provided they work as much, and in identical conditions, and younger learners.

The main reason children learn faster is that we don't judge them nearly as hard as we judge other adults who are learning language. When we hear a kid pronounce his first word, we are amazed. Yet, would you be amazed if you heard an adult French tourist say "hello"? Probably not.

As an adult, you already know at least one language, English. You know how to read, write, and speak. You know what sentences and verbs are. You understand that some words can have different pronunciations and that the pronunciation of a word doesn't always match the way it's written. That's a huge advantage. Unlike a child, you don't have to learn everything from scratch; you already know a lot.

For example, you don't have to learn the alphabet, because you already know it. A kid would need months to be able to read in French. Sure, you won't read with the correct pronunciation, but you can read, and this makes learning much easier. Try to learn Japanese or any another Asian language and you will see what I am talking about.

As an adult, you also have the ability to find patterns. You would quickly notice similarities between the way sentences are constructed in French and in English. Take the following sentence for example:

He is cute.
Il est mignon.

Without even speaking French fluently, you can see the similarities between the two sentences. They both start with the pronoun ("he" in English, "il" in French), followed by the verb ("is" in English, "est" in French) and end with the adjective ("cute" in English, "mignon" in French).

You can also notice the dot at the end of both sentences, and you know it means the sentence has ended. A kid learning his mother tongue wouldn't notice all of that; he would have to learn it all from the beginning. Neither would a kid know that a comma marks a pause. In fact, a kid wouldn't be able to read that sentence at all in the beginning. These are things we take for granted because they seem so obvious, but we forget it hasn't always been the case.

One part is true though, it is harder for an adult learner to acquire a perfect pronunciation, because the adult brain doesn't notice the differences of sounds as easily as a kid's brain. But more difficult doesn't mean impossible, and countless French learners can prove it. You can acquire a perfect French accent if you work hard and use the right techniques. In fact, you are going to discover how to do this in the chapter dedicated to pronunciation.

The other, and probably main advantage, kids have is that they simply don't care about what people think. They are not afraid to sound ridiculous and to make mistakes. When they do, someone corrects them and they learn from it.

Adults, on the other hand, are often terrified at the idea of making mistakes. All too often, the idea that other people will judge us is so scary that we prefer to remain silent rather than take the risk and make a mistake. That's extremely damaging when you are trying to learn a language. As a French proverb says, "forging makes a blacksmith." If you don't speak and accept that you will make mistakes, you can't get feedback, and making progress without feedback makes learning much harder.

Imagine what it would have been like if, as a kid, you had been afraid to speak for the first time. If that had been the case, you probably wouldn't speak any language at all now. Every parent looks forward to hearing his kid speak for the first time. There is a good reason for that; we all know intuitively that the only way to seriously learn a language is to speak it.

You are an adult now, so your brain naturally tells you that you should be afraid to be ridiculous and to make mistakes. But if you truly want to learn French, you will need to make mistakes, and you will need to be ridiculous sometimes. This is something you should accept right now, because it is essential.

In most situations, acting like a kid isn't necessarily a good thing, but when it comes to speaking French, this is the best thing you could do. And don't forget that if a kid can learn French, you can, too.

You need lots of money to learn a language

The person who told you that was most likely trying to sell you something like a $600 language-learning software maybe? Truth is, most language-learning resources are free, or if not free, then very inexpensive.

From my experience, spending lots of money on language-learning software is often just a way to feel good about yourself. I mean, since you just spent $300 on language-learning software, isn't it the ultimate proof of your dedication to learning French? Won't you be super motivated after spending so much money? Sadly (or maybe fortunately), it doesn't work like that.

Language-learning software is not priced based on value. The companies creating language-learning software make the programs so expensive just because they can and because they know that a high price tag gives the consumer the wrong impression that after buying the software, everything will be easy. It almost feels like you won't even need to learn the language once you buy the software. And that's what often happens.

You buy the software and you feel good about it. You use it for one or two weeks and then you stop. You bought it hoping it will make you fluent in French, so you expect it to work, but sadly, even after spending all that money, it doesn't work the way you expect.

There are ways to make the learning process easier; there are software programs that make learning French much more enjoyable. But there is no software that will magically make you fluent in French. Whatever software or language course you choose, you will need to work hard and practice.

If someone ever promises that you can be fluent in French in 7 days, run away! You should only spend money on a language-learning tool if you feel this tool can truly help you. Too many language learners act like collectors, feeling the need to buy three grammar books, four vocabulary books, and two language-learning software programs. If you know you won't use the software, then waste your money. The same goes for books or anything else related to learning French.

Buying language-learning software can be an excellent idea; it can help you get into a learning routine and learn French faster without always having to wonder what to do next. The right program can also give you access to a teacher or a community willing to help you and answer your questions. But before you buy anything to learn French, ask yourself the following questions: Do you really need it? What will it help you achieve? And only buy software if you are absolutely certain it will be useful. Otherwise, you will end up with software or a course you will never use.

Some companies claim that you can "learn French in 10 days" with their software. Unfortunately, you can't. I would love to be able to tell you the contrary, but I can't.

You can start learning French in 10 days, or learn how to introduce yourself in French in 10 days. You can even learn enough to have a basic conversation, but you can't become fluent in French in a week.

In fact, you don't even need to spend money to learn French; you can find all the free resources you need on the internet. There is a catch though. Free French courses generally are not as well-organized and as high-quality as paid resources. So you can definitely save lots of money and learn French for free, but this will most likely make the learning process slower. If you have money, investing in the right French course can save you time and make your learning experience easier.

I will tell you about my favorite French courses later in this book. I will also show you how you can learn French for free if that is what you want to do. In either case, you will end up with all you need to successfully learn French.

Learning French is difficult

When you tell people you are learning French, their first reaction is often along the lines of "wow, you are so brave, good luck." That's because people consider French difficult, when it really isn't all that difficult for native English speakers. The difficulty of a language depends a lot on the languages you already speak. As an English speaker, you already know the alphabet used in French, and you understand the similar sentence structure. When I was teaching French in Korea, I noticed that students had a hard time knowing in what order to put the words. This is a problem you won't have, or at least not as much, since you already speak English. You won't need to learn the Latin alphabet either, lucky you!

According to the Foreign Service Institute (FSI) of the US Department of State, because of its similarity with English, French is one of the easiest languages for a native English speaker to learn. They estimate that you could reach the level 3 of the ILR scale, which is the ability to speak the language with sufficient structural accuracy and vocabulary to participate effectively in most conversations on practical, social, and professional topics, after just 24 weeks, or roughly 600 hours.

If you study one hour per day, you would be fluent in French after a little less than two years. If you study three hours per day, you would be fluent in eight months. If this sounds like a lot to you, remember that these are only estimates based on the time it takes for most students to learn French. You could learn faster if you use the right tools and techniques.

The key to learning French fast is to focus on the similarities rather than the differences between French and English. For example, did you know that up to one third of English words come from French? Since you speak English, you already know hundreds of French words without being aware of it. In fact, you probably use French words on a regular basis. Here are some words that are identical or nearly identical in French and in English:

- Words ending in -tion (communication, information, competition, justification, action…).
- Words with a circumflex. The circumflex (^) is the sign that a "s" used to follow a vowel in French (forêt VS forest, hôpital VS hospital…).
- Words related to food (menu, à la carte, picnic, salade, soupe…).
- Adverbs in -ly. The "ly" part becomes "ement" in French. (rapidly VS rapidement, delicately VS délicatement…).
- And much more…

All the words above are common French words, yet I am sure you easily recognized them. There are hundreds more French words you already know, and this can greatly help you when you start learning French. You don't have to learn everything from scratch.

Now, I won't deny that French grammar and pronunciation can be scary, but they are not as hard to master as you think. Once you are familiar with the sounds of the French language, pronouncing words suddenly becomes easy. And once you are used to the pattern in pronunciation and grammar, you can successfully guess the pronunciation, conjugation, and grammar in the majority of cases.

Chapter Two
The golden rules of language learning

You must work hard

Even though learning French isn't that hard and I believe everyone can succeed, you still need to follow a few rules in order to successfully learn French. These are simple rules, yet many learners neglect them and then don't understand why they don't learn faster.

The first of these rules is to work hard. This is something I mentioned a few times already, but I feel it's important to insist on the matter. Because this is the number one rule to successfully learn French. If you don't work hard, you won't succeed.

Many companies promise you can "learn French in 10 days" or learn without any effort. This is simply not true. As a result of hearing this, many language learners get discouraged when they don't learn easily or fast. After one month, they realize they didn't learn as much as they would have liked, and so they think there is something wrong with them and give up.

There is nothing fundamentally hard about learning French, but it takes time and you won't see results immediately. In order to be successful, you need to be ready to work regularly. You will need to make a real effort to learn French, but making an effort and working hard doesn't mean it should be boring. In fact, I encourage you to have as much fun as possible when learning French.

Nothing great can happen if you don't make it happen. You can learn French fast and have fun, but you need to make it happen. This may sound silly, but many French learners expect to magically learn French without doing much of anything in the process. Wanting to learn French is essential, but the desire is useless if you don't actually spend time learning French.

Working hard means doing your best to learn French as fast as possible. It doesn't mean doing boring tasks and learning grammar rules by heart. There are many entertaining ways to learn French, and one of the goals of this book is precisely to help you find your favorite way to learn French.

Regularity is essential

The second common pattern found among successful language learners is regularity. A daily 15 minute session works better than a weekly three hour session.

This is because our memory considers that what we don't regularly review isn't important, and therefore the information doesn't stay in our memory. Studying daily prevents you from forgetting and makes learning French a habit, something as natural as taking a shower or brushing your teeth.

I totally understand that you may not want to study French after an exhausting day of work. Luckily, there are many ways to study. You could listen to a dialogue and repeat what you hear; you could write something in French and then post it in an online community to get corrections; or you could watch funny videos in French.

If you feel that what you are doing becomes boring or if you are too tired, do something else instead. There is nothing wrong with watching a movie if you just came back home after an exhausting day. Rest is essential to the cognitive process. Without rest, your brain cannot memorize anything.

But instead of watching a movie in English like you usually do, try watching a movie in French. This will require less energy than reading or learning vocabulary, but will still be extremely beneficial in helping you remember what you are learning. You will learn how to pronounce French words, discover new words, and even learn how to use words you already know.

If you study French a little bit every day, no matter how tired you are, you will make progress quickly. You may think that you don't have enough time to learn French, but this is rarely true. Most of us spend quite a lot of time every day waiting. Think about how much time you spend waiting for someone, waiting for the train, waiting in the doctor's office, waiting in line in the grocery store, waiting in traffic jams during rush hour.

You can easily use your daily commute to learn French, or you can learn French while waiting during various times during the day or during the week. If you really don't have time, even during your daily commute, why not take ten minutes before sleeping to study French. Sure, spending so little time learning French will make the process slower, but you will improve a little every day, and one day, you will realize you speak French much better than you thought.

Here are 4 ways to study French in 10 minutes or less:

- Recall vocabulary (see the chapter about vocabulary).
- Watch a short TV series or video (you can find great videos here).
- Read a short text.
- Write about your day (see the chapter about writing).

To do: Try to find a few minutes (or hours) every day to study French.

Don't forget to have fun

Unless you absolutely have to learn French for a class or maybe for your job, you will give up if you don't enjoy the learning process. That's why you shouldn't look for THE best way to learn French; you should look for YOUR best way to learn French, means finding the way to learn French and enjoy the process. Do you love to watch movies? Or are you more the reading type? Or perhaps you prefer to go out and talk to people. Whatever your passion is, you can use it to learn French.

Even the most unrelated passion can be a great learning tool. For example, if you are into gardening, you could start reading French blogs about the subject, or you could watch French documentaries with subtitles. Once you speak French well enough, you could also look for a conversation partner or an online community with people who share your interest in the subject.

Once you find an interesting way to learn French, everything about the process becomes easier. You no longer have to force yourself to study because you will look forward to it. As a result, you make more progress and feel good about it. This is a virtuous circle.

This learning process would never have started had you chosen to learn the conjugation of every French verb in the dictionary by heart (unless that's your thing naturally). In fact, this may have happened to you at school. Your teacher asked you to learn boring things you didn't want to learn. So you either learned them reluctantly or didn't learn them at all. Either way, you quickly forgot them, and associated French with boring conjugation tables and endless grammar drills. Not the best way to get motivated, is it?

If the first thing that comes to mind when you hear "French" is "boring," then learning will be hard. On the contrary, if learning French makes you think about all the interesting conversations you can have in this language or about a movie you love, learning will be much easier.

Sure, you will need to do some boring tasks in order to learn French, but if you make sure most of the learning process is fun, you greatly improve your chances of success.

To do: Always try to find a fun way to learn French.

Chapter Three
Staying motivated

Why do you want to learn French

Before you even start learning French, take the time to ask yourself the following question: Why do you want to learn French? Is it to get your dream job? Is it because you love French culture? Is it to impress or please someone? Is it simply because it would be nice to speak another language?

Whatever the reason, make sure this reason will keep you motivated in the long term. Almost everyone wants to speak another language fluently, but few people actually end up speaking another language fluently. Motivation is one of the main differences between people who end up speaking another language fluently and people who don't.

I often get emails from readers of *French Together* asking whether they should study French, Spanish, or German. And my answer is always the same: Study the language you want to learn the most, because this is also the language you are the most likely to speak fluently at the end. It would be awesome to speak Chinese, but if you aren't motivated to learn it and just want to learn it because "it would be useful," you are unlikely to succeed. It is better to focus all of your energy on one language project.

If, from the beginning, you clearly know why you want to learn French, nothing is going to stop you. And I can promise you will speak French fluently in a matter of months or years depending on the time you can invest.

Once you have a clear idea of why you want to learn French, it's time to set goals and plan your studies.

To do : write down your motivation for learning French.

Why and how to set goals

Setting goals is extremely important because then you have a clear idea of what to do next. And let's face it, few things are more motivating than crossing goals off your to do list.

One common mistake when it comes to setting goals is to write unclear goals like "become fluent in French." This goal is too vague and too remote to really motivate you. It is extremely hard to motivate yourself and think "I am learning French now in order to speak it fluently within one year." You need a S.M.A.R.T goal:

- Specific
- Measurable
- Attainable
- Realistic
- Time bound

The best way to set such a goal is to start with the bigger goals before creating sub goals. Your big goal could be to be able to have a 15 minute conversation in French before the end of the year. And you could choose sub goals such as:

- Learn how to introduce myself in French.
- Learn how to talk about my passions.
- Write 300 words to introduce myself in French.

These goals are all specific, measurable, attainable, and realistic. But they are not time bound, so you are likely to procrastinate. In order to make sure you realize each of these goals, you need to add a deadline.

You can do that by adding the deadline in your calendar or in your to-do list. Your goal then becomes, for example, "write 300 words to introduce myself in French on Monday," followed by "introduce myself to a native French speaker found on Italki on Tuesday."

You can also set daily goals, such as "read an article in French every day" or "watch TV in French for 30 minutes every day." Unlike S.M.A.R.T goals, daily goals are not necessarily measurable. You can measure the time you spend watching French TV, but you can't measure the effect it has on your French skills. This makes daily goals harder to follow in the long run. Luckily, a few tools can greatly help.

What tools can you use to set your goals?

Since we are talking about daily goals, I recommend you to use Lift.do . This free app allows you to set daily goals and write every day whether or not you achieved those goals. The advantage of *lift.do* over other apps is that you are part of a community of people dedicated to achieving their goals. You can comment on other people's goals, ask for advice and even add friends who will see whether or not you achieve your goals. This holds you accountable, which can be a huge motivation boost.

For your S.M.A.R.T goals, I recommend Todoist.com. You can use Todoist to divide your goals into sub goals, classify your goals by category, and set deadlines. You can even set notifications on your phone to be sure you don't forget about your goals.

To do: Decide in advance what you are going to study and write clear goals.

How to avoid distractions

Let's say you are working on one of your French language goals, perhaps you are learning how to introduce yourself in French. While you're online, you receive a message on Facebook. What do you do? We would all like to answer "ignore it," yet you know as well as I do that this is unlikely.

We are curious by nature. If we receive a message or a notification, not checking it is almost impossible. And even if you don't check it, you will most likely wonder what it's about while you are studying.

This is less than ideal when you are trying to learn anything. That's why you should make sure you can't be distracted when you study French. The best way to achieve that is to get rid of all potential distractions. Here are some ideas:

- Turn off your phone, tablet etc.
- Turn off the TV or any other source of noise (unless you use music or white noise to focus).
- Hide other devices so you are not tempted to turn them on.
- Go somewhere where nobody will distract you.
- Install a software program that blocks distracting websites.
- Set a timer.

These steps all have the same goal, which is to make it as hard as possible for you to be distracted. If your phone or tablet is on, you will be tempted to check your messages. This won't happen if it's off and hidden, because we tend to prefer the easy way. If you have to turn on your phone in order to check your messages, you are less likely to do it, because it simply requires more effort.

Similarly, keeping your phone out of sight helps you forget about it. Think about a delicious chocolate cake. If it's in front of you, you will remember how starving you are every time you see it; if it's hidden, you may sometimes think about it, but not as often.

Since you will probably use a computer to study French, it's important to take precautions and make sure you won't be tempted to visit Facebook "just for one minute." Here are a few apps that block access to distracting websites like Facebook, Twitter, and Reddit :

Macfreedom (paid app: Mac, Windows, Android, Macfreedom.com).
Leechblock (free: firefox, frenchtogether.com/go/leechblock).
Self Control App (free: Mac only, frenchtogether.com/go/self-control).

These apps will prevent you from visiting websites or some will block your internet access depending on how you configure them. And if you ever want to deactivate them, you will need to reboot your computer. This should be enough to keep you focused.

In addition to all of these precautions, I recommend that you use the Pomodoro technique named after the word pomodoro (tomato in Italian). This technique is simple: you use a timer to create short learning sessions of 25 minutes, with short breaks between each session. I can't tell you why it works so well. What I can tell you is that I work much faster and get much more done now that I use it. So give it a try. Here is a free timer you can use:

http://tomato-timer.com

Chapter Four
All you need to know about immersion

You don't need to live in France to learn French

The fact that a French-speaking country is the ideal place to learn French doesn't mean that you absolutely need to go to a French-speaking country to learn French. In fact, I only spent two weeks of my life in an English-speaking country, yet I consider my English to be fluent. There are many other examples of people who speak a language fluently without ever going to the country where that language is spoken. Where you are doesn't matter as long as you are motivated. And what you do matters much more than where you do it.

What you need is an immersion environment, which is an environment in which you are as exposed to the French language as possible. The idea is to make the French language an important part of your life so that you can't help but learn it. Want to read news? Why not do it in French? Feel like watching a movie? See if you can find the French version.

As a beginner, you may have a hard time switching to French for some activities at first. Reading a book in French when you barely speak the language can be tedious. That's why it's important to immerse yourself progressively. If, all of a sudden, you go from everything in English to everything in French, you will not understand any of the French and you'll easily become frustrated.

You can start by changing the language of your phone, Facebook and email accounts. You probably use them every day; you are familiar with them and changing the language won't prevent you from using them. After a few days, you won't even notice the new language anymore, but you will learn some useful vocabulary just by using them in French rather than English. Most importantly, you will get used to the idea of speaking French and will want to study more.

Once you are used to the new language of your devices and accounts, think about all the activities you could do in French rather than English. An easy start is to listen to French music instead of the usual artists you listen to. This doesn't require much energy and allows you to get more familiar with the sound of the French language. At this stage, it doesn't matter whether you understand the lyrics or not; it's all about getting your brain used to the way words and sentences are spoken in French.

The same is true for movies. When you start learning French, watching a movie or TV series with subtitles is a good solution. The goal is to get used to the language. You don't need to be actively watching because your brain will naturally pick up vocabulary and associate the subtitles you read with the sounds you hear. As soon as you start building your vocabulary, you will be able to identify more and more words in the movies you watch and songs you listen to.

As a kid, you learned your native language by listening a lot first, then you repeated what you heard and started creating sentences. After a while, you learned how to write, studied basic grammar rules and started reading. In other words, you started with a passive listening phase, before becoming active and talking.

Once you know a few sentences and have an idea of how to pronounce and write French words and sentences, the active phase begins. The precise moment at which this active phase should begin is a controversial topic in the language learning community. Some swear that you should "speak from day one," while others prefer to wait to have a large vocabulary before speaking. I advise you to speak as soon as possible because that's the best way to know when you make mistakes and to see if your pronunciation is correct. You will learn and remember more words and sentences by actively using them.

If you feel you are not ready to talk to someone yet, you can start by writing something using the words and sentences you know, and then read it out loud once you made sure what you wrote is correct (cf: how to get corrections from native speakers). This is not as effective as talking to a native speaker because you don't know whether or not your pronunciation is correct. But you at least get used to speaking and using the vocabulary you learned.

To sum up, you don't need to be in a French-speaking country to learn French. You need input and output. You get the input by reading and listening to a lot of French, while you get the output by speaking and writing. The more input and output you have, the closer you get to fluency.

Living in France is not enough to speak French

We all like to think that we will suddenly become fluent in a language once we live in the country where it's spoken. Wouldn't it be great? You would be able to automatically learn French while discovering the country, eating delicious food and having fun. After one year in France, you would go back home and amaze everyone around you.

Look, I hate to be the one to tell you, but this is not going to happen.

Being in the country where the language you learn is spoken helps a lot, no doubt about that. If you live in France, you get to hear people speak French all the time, everything is written in French, and you can easily practice your French all the time. This is ideal for immersion. Despite all that, many French learners barely improve their French after a few months in France. Why? Because what you need is input and output, and living in France is not enough. Living in France won't automatically make you fluent in French. Actually, you can live in France and still speak French very rarely, talk to other foreigners in English, only read English books and watch English movies and TV series.

Instead of simply living in France, you need to become French for a few months. You need to speak French, read in French and do everything you can in French. When you move to a foreign country and don't speak the language, you feel lonely and you don't understand what people around you say, so looking for people who speak your language is natural. It is also a huge mistake. If you want to learn the language, you need to avoid people who speak your own language. If you start making English-speaking friends, you will quickly find yourself speaking English all the time, and that would ruin your immersion in the French language.

This is what happened to me when I lived in Berlin in 2012. I moved there with an American friend, thinking "my friend is American, but it doesn't matter, because when I am not with her, I will only speak German." Three months later, my German had barely improved. Since my roommate spoke English, I was speaking English all the time at home. I was also speaking English when I went out with her. As a result, many of the people I met were people who only spoke English. And so I ended up spending most of my time in Germany speaking English instead of German. Sure, I occasionally spoke German at the supermarket and got very good at saying "hi" in German, but apart from that, I wasted my time.

The problem was that it was easier for me to speak English than German since most of my friends only spoke English. Sure, I could have gone out and met some German people, but this meant going out of my comfort zone and I endlessly procrastinated. Every day, I told myself that I would do it the next day. At the end, I never did it. I even ended up speaking English with most of the German people I met. Why? Because it was easier. I would start speaking in German and would eventually get frustrated and switch to English. Once that was done, going back to German was extremely difficult.

The first time you speak to someone in French, you too will get frustrated. You will have plenty of things to say and not enough words to express your thoughts. This will be even more frustrating if you find your conversation partner interesting. There is nothing more frustrating than wanting to talk to someone and not be able to do so. You shouldn't give up, though. Whenever you feel the desire to switch to English, remember why you are speaking French, and remember that if you keep speaking French you will eventually get the reward of fluency.

Your conversation partner may want to switch to English at some point; after all, he too may want to improve his knowledge of a foreign language. In this case, you should, of course, do it. But make sure you don't end up speaking English all the time. A good way to avoid that is to set a timer. You have 15 minutes to speak French, then 15 minutes to speak English, then 15 minutes to speak French again, etc.

Some language exchange meetings make it easier for you to practice French by strictly forbidding the use of your native language. In such meetings, you will only be allowed to use the language you are learning. If you don't do that, other people will remind you. We will talk about ways to find such meetings in the chapter dedicated to speaking.

Chapter Five
*How to learn French grammar
without going crazy*

Don't learn it!

Many people find French extremely difficult because they focus too much on grammar. When you start learning French, you don't need to know much about grammar. It's good to know that some words are feminine and other masculine and to know how to conjugate the different group of verbs, but obsessing about it will slow you down, if not stop you completely.

Sure, you will make mistakes at first, but this is not a problem. Nobody will blame you for using "le" instead of "la." And frankly, it won't prevent anyone from understanding you. I often meet tourists who try to speak French and make mistakes, and I don't think "wow they make so many mistakes." Instead, I think "they are trying hard to speak my language; it's good and I want to help them."

If you try to learn French grammar rules by heart, you will be overwhelmed when you find out how many exceptions there are. French people often joke that there are more exceptions than rules, and unfortunately, this is sometimes true. Does it mean you will never master French grammar? No, this means you should not try to. When you stumble upon sentence construction you don't understand or a verb conjugation you don't know, search for answers, try to understand how the sentence is constructed and the verb conjugated, but don't obsess over it. Simply try to understand how it works, and you will quickly improve your understanding of French grammar.

This approach will prevent frustration and allow you to learn grammar naturally, the same way native French speakers did. Think about it, how did you learn English grammar? Did you learn all the rules by heart, or did you simply learn automatically after hearing and reading lots of English? As a native English speaker, you intuitively know whether a sentence is grammatically correct or not, but could you explain why a sentence is right or wrong? Not always. This is because you intuitively know grammar, and that's what you should try to do in French.

It may sound counter-intuitive, but the best way to learn French grammar is to not study it. If you get enough input by reading and listening in French, your brain will do something amazing. It will analyze all the sentences you read and hear, notice patterns and memorize their construction. On the contrary, if you try to learn all the textbook grammar rules by heart, you will fall asleep.

The more input you have, the greater you will become at forming sentences and understanding the language. However, this doesn't mean that you should never look up grammar rules. If you regularly stumble upon a sentence whose construction you don't understand, reading about the related grammar rule is an excellent idea. It can actually save you lots of time.

For example, with enough input, you would automatically learn to distinguish feminine and masculine words, but it will take a while before you know enough words to be able to identify the gender of a word just by looking at it. In this case, it is wise to take a look at a list of the gender of words based on their ending. This is what I call a grammar hack, something you can look up that will immediately help you speak French better using common patterns in the language.

According to a study by Mcgill University, a French word's ending indicates its gender in 80% of cases. This makes learning French genders much easier, because you have a simple way to know the gender of a word just by looking at its ending.

Typically masculine word endings (+90%)

- -an, -and, -ant, -ent, -in, -int, -om, -ond, -ont, -on (but not after s/c$_s$)
- -eau, -au, -aud, -aut, -o, -os, -ot
- -ai, -ais, -ait, -es, -et
- -ou, -out, -out, -oux
- -i, -il, -it, -is, -y
- -at, -as, -ois, -oit
    - -u, -us, -ut, -eu
- -er, -e´after C (C=t)
- -age, -ege, – ` eme, -ome/- ` ome, -aume, -isme
- -as, -is, -os, -us, -ex

51

- -it, -est
- -al, -el, -il, -ol, -eul, -all
- -if, -ef
- -ac, -ic, -oc, -uc
- -am, -um, -en
- -air, -er, -erf, -ert, -ar, -arc, -ars, -art, -our, -ours, -or, -ord, -ors, -ort, -ir, -oir, -eur
  (if animate)
- -ail, -eil, -euil, -ueil
- -ing

Typically feminine word endings (+90%)

- -aie, -oue, -eue, -ion, -te, − ´ ee, -ie, -ue
- -asse, -ace, -esse, -ece, -aisse, -isse/-ice, -ousse, -ance, -anse, -ence, -once
- -enne, -onne, -une, -ine, -aine, -eine, -erne
- -ande, -ende, -onde, -ade, -ude, -arde, -orde
- -euse, -ouse, -ase, -aise, -ese, -oise, -ise, -yse, -ose, -use
- -ache, -iche, -eche, -oche, -uche, -ouche, -anche
- -ave, -eve, -ive
- -iere, -ure, -eure
- -ette, -ete, − ˆ ete, -atte, -otte, -oute, -orte, -ante, -ente, -inte, -onte
- -alle, -elle, -ille, -olle

- -aille, -eille, -ouille
- -appe, -ampe, -ombe
- -igue

Since this book is not about grammar, you won't find any more grammar hacks here. I invite you to subscribe to *My French Together (frenchtogether.com/my-french-together)* for free to be informed whenever I post a new article. You can also receive a weekly selection of the best content from the web. These selections often include great grammar hacks.

Chapter Six
What material do you need to learn French

Less is more

I encourage you not to buy too many courses and books. In fact, you only need two things to get started learning French: a great French course and a good grammar book.

You are super motivated and you want to learn French as fast as possible, I get it. But if you buy too many books and courses, you will end up facing the paradox of choice. You will have too many choices that you could become confused and not know what to choose. When it comes to learning French, less is more.

You don't need two grammar books or three French courses. If you have too many options, you will lose time every day wondering which to use, when the most important thing to do is to actually learn French in the first place. This is all the more important if you can only spend a few minutes per day learning French.

A great French course doesn't have to be fancy. All you need to have good is dialogues with audio (that's the first input you will receive). This may seem basic, but this can actually be quite hard to find. Many courses use old-fashioned French, or the kind of sentences you will never use if you were speaking in France. What you are looking for is a course using real everyday French. Here are a few options:

Assimil (assimil.com):This French course was created by a French company. It contains high-quality dialogues, great recordings and basic grammar explanations. This is one of the best and cheapest courses; however, since it's simply made, with a book and recordings, you will need to find a way to stay motivated on your own. This is awesome if you like to learn on your own, but if you prefer to feel you are part of a community, a course like *Babbel* would be better for you.

Babbel (babbel.com): More than a course, *Babbel* is an online community of learners. You will find high-quality dialogues, recordings, a SRS tool and you can also contact other members and find a French conversation partner this way. This will give you less flexibility than *Assimil* but would be better for you if you like to feel part of a community.

Duolingo (duolingo.com): This free website adopts a different approach. Instead of dialogues and sentences, *Duolingo* asks you to translate the web. During each lesson, the website teaches new words and sentences that you will then be asked to translate. This can be an effective way to improve your French if you like translating.

You can also learn French using a list of the most common French words. The advantage of this is that you will learn the most useful French words and will quickly be able to understand French. The disadvantage is that since there is no such list available with audio yet, you will have to create one. You can become a member of *My*

French Together for free and receive a list of the 100 most common French words with example sentences.

There are several ways you could be using your French course. If you chose *Assimil*, you will see that each lesson contains a dialogue and a recording. You can first listen to the dialogue and try to understand as much as possible. Then you can read and listen at the same time. Finally, you can look at the translation and enter each useful sentence in your SRS software.

If you chose *Babbel*, the SRS software is already integrated and the software will guide you through the learning journey. Whether you chose *Babbel, Assimil* or another course, don't forget to review vocabulary every day in your SRS software. Studying will become a habit and you will always review sentences before you forget them. Don't worry if you don't know what SRS software is – this is something you will soon discover in more detail. To summarize, SRS allows you to study vocabulary and review it before you are about to forget it.

Once you start studying with a course, you will tend to easily forget the other aspects of learning French. The French course provides you with input, but you also need output to learn French. In order to get the output you need, you can spend the first half of your time using your course and the second doing something else. For example, you could start by doing a lesson and then write in French or talk to someone in French. If you are not ready for that, you could also read something or watch a video in French, with or without subtitles, depending on your level.

In addition to a French course, you will also need to choose a grammar book. You don't have to do it immediately, because your course probably includes some basic grammar explanations. This is the case with *Assimil* and *Babbel*. These explanations should be enough to get started. However, if this is not enough, *Google* is often your best friend. I find that googling a problem often gives you all the answers you need. You can also check *www.french.about.com*. In case you prefer a physical grammar book, *French Grammar: A Complete Reference Guide* has many positive reviews.

Chapter Seven
How to learn vocabulary and never forget it

Learning the right words

You take a list of words and read them out loud, again and again. After ten minutes, you are already bored and after 20 minutes, you stop. Three days later, you realize you don't remember anything.

This is what I like to call the parrot method. This is boring and ineffective. Yet, this is the most common way to learn vocabulary. Of course, you will remember a few words, but for how long? When you learn new words, it's important to ask yourself the following questions:

Why am I learning this word?
Will I ever use it?

There is no point in learning a useless word. If you think you are never going to use a word, don't learn it!

A dictionary like *Le Grand Robert de la Langue Française* contains 100,000 words and 350,000 definitions. Your goal as a French learner shouldn't be to learn them all. What you want to know is the most useful words, the words you will need once the time to speak French has come. These words will differ depending on the reason you want to learn French. Someone working in IT won't need to know the same words as a student who is going to France for vacations.

There are a few words that will always be useful to everyone; these are the most common words. By learning these words first, you are certain that every word you learn is one that you will use and hear when you go to France. In English, these would be words like "the," "be," or "to." Hard to imagine a conversation without them, isn't it?

To make it easy for you to learn these, I have created a list of the 100 most common French words. You can get this list for free by joining *My French Together (frenchtogether.com/my-french-together)*. In addition to the most common French words, this list also contains example sentences. This is essential as you will discover in the next pages.

How to make words memorable

What if you could learn words and never forget them? Wouldn't that be awesome? Well, the good news is, you can. Contrary to a common myth, there is almost never such thing as a bad memory. If you eat well, sleep well, and don't suffer from a memory-related disease, you too can have a great memory and remember words and sentences easily. All you need to do is apply techniques you can easily implement in your daily life to considerably boost your ability to memorize anything, be it the name of a person you met at a party, or a new French word.

You need to make words important

When you are bored, tired or don't want to do something, you generally don't pay much attention to what you are doing. If you repeat a word out loud and think about something else at the same time, you are unlikely to remember this word a few hours a later. That's because our world is so huge our memory cannot remember everything, so it has to be selective and only chooses to remember what it considers important. When you are bored or don't pay attention to a word you are trying to learn, you trick your memory into thinking that word is useless and boring. As a result, you forget it.

You know you shouldn't touch fire, because it would burn you. You also know the meaning of "mom" or "dad" because these are two words you needed a lot as a kid.

Most words seem unimportant at first and it's your role to make each and every word you want to learn important so that it sticks in your memory. Don't worry; it's much easier than it sounds.

Let me ask you a question now: can you remember 5 commercials or ads? What do they have in common? We see hundreds of commercials and ads every month, yet only a few of them stick in our memory. The same thing happens with words. In order to learn words effectively, you need to know what makes them memorable.

There are many factors of course, but usually we remember:

- What shocked us
- What surprised us
- What made us laugh
- What we consider important
- What we saw or heard a lot

Basically, everything that is the opposite of boring. To remember a word or sentence, you need to make it special and then review it regularly.

How to make a word special

If you are like the majority of learners, you probably just take each word, translate it, write it on a paper or on your computer, and read it again more or less regularly. There are multiple problems with this approach.

First, it's boring. Second, you don't create any personal connection with the word, so you have nothing to help you remember it. Finally, you don't recall the word, you simply review it. By doing this, you don't make any effort. You see the word and think "yeah I knew it" or "nooooo I have been trying to memorize this word for two hours, how come I can't memorize it!" In both cases, since you don't make the conscious effort to recall the meaning of the word, your memory considers this word useless and puts it in the "to forget soon" category.

Think about it; how much of what you learned in high school do you remember? I left high school three years ago, yet if I had to take the exam again, I would probably fail. Why? Because I learned everything by heart just before the exam and forgot everything just after the exam. This works to pass exams (although I don't recommend this method), but you won't go very far if you apply it to language learning.

The other reason you don't remember anything you learned in high school is that you never reviewed it after leaving high school. When you learn a language, you need to regularly recall words, otherwise you forget them. We quickly forget words we don't try to remember. This is called the forgetting curve.

According to Hermann Ebbinghaus, the German psychologist who discovered the forgetting curve, two elements can greatly improve our ability to remember: mnemonics (what I call associations) and repetitions based on active recall, which are repetitions where you force yourself to remember something. This is something you will learn to do at the end of this chapter.

Creating associations to better remember words

Hermann Ebbinghaus found that mnemonics greatly improve our chances to remember. This is because our memory doesn't store information in one single place. When you create mnemonics or associations, you connect the word to something you already know and make it easier to access and therefore easier to remember. The more associations you create, the easier it is to remember a word.

If I tell you the word "food," lots of images probably cross your mind. You imagine your favorite dish; you may even suddenly want to eat (sorry about that). The word creates a reaction in your brain. This is because you associate the word food with many experiences or even feelings. But what if I tell you the word "papillon"? Chances are nothing crosses your mind. You don't have any connection with this word. Worse, you probably don't even know its meaning.

If you just opened a dictionary, you found that "papillon" is the French word for "butterfly." Do you think you will remember that within three days? Maybe. Within one week? Less likely. Within one month? Probably not. You could repeat papillon = butterfly out loud for ten minutes, and it would slightly increase the chances of remembering its meaning.

Or you could associate the word "papillon" with a memory, a similar sound, a picture, a feeling, and remember it forever. I could give you a mnemonic to remember "papillon," but it wouldn't be doing you a favor. This is because the strongest associations are personal ones, associations linked with your memories, your experiences, your knowledge. And you are the only one able to create them.

If I had to learn the Korean word "nuna" (older sister), I would simply write the name of a friend I used to call "nuna" and this would be enough for me to never forget the meaning of this word because the emotional impact of it is extremely strong...for me. If I give you a card with this written, it won't help you at all. In fact, you wouldn't even guess the meaning.

That's the reason why many language learning software programs don't work nearly as well as you expect them to. They often show you pictures along with words and sometimes even write jokes or mnemonics to help you remember words. But these are not YOUR jokes, YOUR mnemonics or YOUR connections.

When you learn the word "enfant," they show you the picture of a child, and this is a good start. But this will never work as well as a picture of your own child, or a picture of a child you know. When you see the picture of a child you know, you feel an emotional connection, and this helps you remember. When you see a random picture, you understand the concept of "enfant" and it helps, but not as much.

Next time you want to learn a word, type the French word in Google images or any other image search engine and try to guess its meaning. Then open a dictionary (http://www.wordreference.com/ is great) and check the meaning of the word. Finally, pick a picture. This can be any picture, but the best is a picture you feel a connection with.

For example, if after typing "chien" (dog), you stumble upon the picture of a dog you find incredibly cute. Choose this picture because it will help you memorize the word. If you are a fan of mangas, typing "chien manga" and selecting a picture of dog in a manga style would work even better.

Once you have found a picture, think about what comes to your mind when you hear the word. It may remind you of something or someone, or the sound could make you think about another word in another language. Whichever the case, write it down. The more associations you have, the easier it is to remember the word.

You may think that looking for a picture is a waste of time, but the benefits of adding an association to a word you learn are so huge that you will quickly make up for the lost time. The time you lost finding a picture and associations is time you will gain when the time to memorize the word will come.

How to use a SRS software

Associations (called mnemonics by Ebbinghaus) are the first element you can use to effectively memorize vocabulary, but the German psychologist found that a second element also has a lot of importance: repetitions using active recall.

The first is relatively easy, but the second can quickly become complicated. As long as you only learned a few words, regularly recalling them isn't a problem. But what happens when you know hundreds or thousands of words (this will happen sooner than you think)? Should you go through all your words and recall them every day? This would be pretty unpractical. That's the reason clever folks created Spaced Repetition Systems.

A Spaced Repetition System (SRS) is a system where you are regularly presented with a word and have to guess its meaning. Then, you regularly recall the word to see if you remember its meaning. But instead of randomly recalling it when you feel like it, the SRS chooses the best time for your review session. The best time is immediately before you forget the word. That's when studies have proven that recalling a word was the most effective.

Imagine a video game where you go from one level to another as you gain experience; in a SRS, each word gains a level every time you successfully recall that word. When you don't recall the word, it loses a level or even goes back to level 1. When a word reaches the final level, that word is in your long-term memory and you normally won't forget it anymore. The better you know a word, the less often you have to recall it. On the other hand, the less you know a word, the more often you need to recall it.

Learners using a SRS system typically know many more words than those who don't. And reviewing all your words generally won't take more than 30 minutes per day. This is the perfect way to spend your daily commute.

What's the best SRS software?

There are lots of SRS software programs on the market, but we are going to focus on the most famous, *Anki*. This is one of the most powerful programs. It's not exactly user-friendly, but don't let that scare you; you will quickly get used to it. *Anki* is available for Windows, Mac OSX, Linux, IOS and Android. All versions are free except the IOS version.

You could also use *Memrise,* which is an online community of learners, You can learn pretty much anything using a flashcard system. Unlike *Anki,* you don't have to create your cards but simply choose a deck among the thousands of decks available. Some decks even have audio integrated. Choosing a pre-made deck won't be as effective as creating one though.

The choice between the two SRS programs is a matter of personal preference. *Anki* is more robust and gives you more options, while *Memrise* is more user-friendly. Beginners often start with *Memrise* before switching to *Anki* at some point to have more freedom. Once you have chosen your SRS software, you can start adding words and, even better, sentences. Even better, you can add pictures and associations.

The importance of context

If you read carefully, you likely noticed that I said adding sentences is better than adding words. That's because learning words in isolation has many disadvantages:

- You don't know how to use the word.
- It's harder to memorize a single word.
- You don't learn grammar.
- You can't distinguish between the different meanings of a word.

On the contrary, learning sentences instead of words has some advantages:

- You immediately know how to use the word.
- You learn a sentence you can use later.
- You learn grammar and conjugation by observing the structure of each sentence.

That's why I recommend that you always learn sentences rather than words. In your SRS software, instead of simply entering the word and its translation, enter a sentence, its translation, and a picture or personal connection which helps you remember the meaning. You can also enter the audio if you have it, and add a quick grammar note, which helps you understand the way the sentence is constructed.

Here is an example :

Le lama crache sur la voiture.
The lama spits on the car.

As a personal connection, you could imagine that the car crashes as a result. Here the English verb "to crash" helps you remember "cracher." Now you are much more likely to remember the meaning of the word "cracher." And if you don't remember, thinking about the car crashing after someone spits on it will help you remember.

This is an association I invented, but you can make up your own. This can even work better since the personal connection you make can then be attached to a memory or something you care about. There may be some cases when no association comes to mind when you learn a word. Don't spend too much time looking for one; this should come naturally. If it doesn't, don't insist. You can learn perfectly without any associations, which are just here to help you.

If the word you learn is useful, you will often get to use it and read it, so your memory will naturally consider it important and you won't forget it. Sometimes though, you will have a hard time memorizing a word you often see and recall using a SRS. In such cases, feel free to create several cards for the same word so that you will have several occasions to recall and make it easier to memorize the word. This is also something you can do to learn the different meanings of a word and avoid confusion.

Although SRS programs are extremely powerful and can greatly help you learn French, they don't replace all the other elements of language-learning. Simply using a SRS won't make you fluent in French. A language is so much more than a list of words. Speaking French is not only about knowing sentences, it's also knowing when to use them, how to pronounce them right and understanding French culture. That's why immersion is so important. Immersing yourself in the language and culture of the country, helps you learn the language, and understand the history of the country and the way people think.

There is another problem though, when you start learning a foreign language like French. You have no idea how to pronounce the words you see. In some cases, you may be able to guess from your past experience hearing French words. But more often than not, you will either be totally unable to pronounce the word or you will pronounce it wrong. That's why it's essential to know how to pronounce a word before you start learning it.

Take the word "accueillir" for example. If you don't know the basics of French pronunciation, you are likely to have no idea how to pronounce the word and, thus, pronounce it incorrectly. As a result, you will have a hard time learning this word, and if you do succeed in learning it, you will associate it with the wrong pronunciation, which could later lead to confusion.

This doesn't mean your pronunciation should be perfect before you even start learning vocabulary; this means you should know the basics of French pronunciation before anything else. If you have already started learning French and didn't study pronunciation, don't worry; it's never too late. You will discover ways to quickly master French pronunciations in the next chapter of this book.

Chapter Eight
How to master pronunciation

Why and how to learn pronunciation

I won't lie to you, acquiring a native-like pronunciation is hard work. Some even say it's impossible. I thought so too, until I met several foreigners with a perfect French accent. I believe one of the main reasons people think acquiring a perfect accent is impossible, is that once you have a perfect accent, people no longer think you are a foreigner, so they don't know that you actually had to work to get this accent.

If you want to get a good French accent, the first thing you need to do is stop using simplified French pronunciations. Using simplified pronunciation made for English speakers may sound like a good idea because you won't have to work hard to know how to pronounce the word. Unfortunately, nobody will ever understand you if you pronounce "pardon" (excuse me) "par-dawn." The last time I heard people speak like that, I actually thought they were making fun of me. Doing this may help you may learn pronunciation faster, but you won't learn French pronunciation; instead, you will learn some kind of Frenglish that nobody else understands.

The other problem is that you get the impression you can pronounce French words with English sounds. While this would be awesome, it isn't really the case. If French and English had the same sounds, pronunciation wouldn't be a problem. The more you use this combination kind of pronunciation, the more you will get used to pronouncing

French words the way you pronounce English words. This is a bad habit you will have a hard time getting rid of. By using a simplified French pronunciation, you actually waste lots of time, because nobody will understand you, and you won't understand people when they use the correct pronunciation. So instead of using this simplified pronunciation, listen to a recording of the correct pronunciation, try to imitate it as well as you can, and learn the IPA.

The IPA (International Phonetic Alphabet) is this strange alphabet you probably learned at school (or were supposed to learn at school if you are like me and thought it was absolutely useless). Learning another alphabet before you learn French may seem like a huge waste of time, but this will actually make you save time because once you know it, you will know how to pronounce French words the right way. This means you will also be able to recognize French words when you hear them.

Since the IPA is based on the Latin alphabet used in English and French, learning it is a rather simple and quick process. Here is a free course you can use to learn the IPA:

frenchtogether.com/go/ipa

Once you know the IPA, you will know the exact pronunciation of each word just by looking at the way the word is written in IPA. This will save you lots of time because you won't mistake similar words anymore and you will quickly get used to French pronunciation. You will instinctively learn to recognize patterns in the way words and sentences are pronounced and will soon be able to guess the pronunciation of an unknown word by just seeing how it's written.

This is something you already do in English actually. If you stumble upon the word "subble," you know how to pronounce it, even though you probably never saw it before since it doesn't exist. There are exceptions, of course, but this will work in the majority of cases. Knowing the IPA and regularly listening to the pronunciation of words you learn will allow you to know how words are pronounced. This won't, however, give you a great pronunciation. Why? Because in order to pronounce sounds, you need to hear these sounds first. And if you are like most people, you cannot hear all the sounds used in French.

A study from the Institute for Learning and Brain Sciences at the University of Washington recently found that monolingual children are able to detect the sounds of two different languages before 10 months, but can no longer do it once they are older than 10 or 12 months. This means that if you grew up as a monolingual child, your brain can no longer distinguish all the sounds of other languages. This can be problematic because it means you could hear two different French words and not hear any difference between them.

It may already have happened to you. You mispronounce a word, so a native speaker kindly repeats the word to help you say it right. The only problem is that you hear no difference between the word you said and the word the native speaker pronounced. For you, these two different sounds are the same. You could hear the word 10 times and still not see the difference.

You are lucky because this won't happen often in French if you are a native English speaker. French and English share lots of common sounds, so most words won't be hard for you to pronounce correctly. If you were learning a language like Russian or Chinese, this would be much more challenging.

And even when this does happen, it will generally not prevent you from being understood by others or from understanding what you hear. However, having a great pronunciation is always a plus. So you will be happy to know that you can teach your brain to recognize the sounds of another language.

How? By bringing immediate feedback to the table. Researchers have found that students who repetitively listened to the same sound didn't improve their ability to recognize it. However, students who heard two different sounds they couldn't distinguish, and were immediately told whether they were right or wrong, were quickly able to make the difference between sounds they couldn't distinguish before.

The English to French pronunciation trainer created by *Fluent Forever* helps you do that. This pronunciation trainer uses *Anki*, the SRS software we mentioned earlier, that was created specifically for native English speakers willing to learn French. After using it, you will be able to recognize all the sounds of the French language. This will make learning the language and most of all pronouncing it correctly much easier.

frenchtogether.com/go/pronunciation-trainer

If you take the time to learn the IPA, use a pronunciation trainer to learn to distinguish French sounds, avoid simplified French pronunciations, and regularly listen to French language, you will quickly be able to speak French without worrying about whether people understand you or not. You may even be mistaken for a native French speaker before you speak the language fluently. This means people will be far less likely to answer you in English when you speak French. The only downside is that people may not realize you are a foreigner, so they will speak fast. But, hey! It's good training!

To do: Learn the IPA, avoid simplified French pronunciations, and learn to recognize French sounds with a pronunciation trainer.

How to find the pronunciation of a word

Once you know the IPA, you can easily find the pronunciation of each word. But what if you want to listen to the pronunciation of the word? Two websites are particularly useful for finding pronunciation recordings of words: *Rhinospike.com* and *Forvo.com*.

Forvo's goal is to have "all the words in the world pronounced." While this goal hasn't yet been reached, the website contains an impressive number of French words. Whenever you want to hear the pronunciation of a word, just go to *forvo.com* and type the word for which you need to hear the pronunciation. Since *Forvo* is based on sharing, you have a much higher chance of getting what you want if you also help in return by recording sentences in your native language.

If this doesn't work or if you want to know how to pronounce a sentence (words can be pronounced differently if they are part of a sentence), head over to *rhinospike.com*. *Rhinospike* provides "language audio on demand." You can go there and ask for the pronunciation of any sentence or word you like.

Once you have your recordings, you can add them to your SRS software so that you can hear them every time you recall a word.

PART TWO
Mastering the four core language skills

Chapter Nine
Reading

How to find the right reading material?

Reading is an essential part of the learning process. When you read, you discover new words, learn how to use the words you already know, and even learn grammar. The last point may be a surprise, but when you read, you get used to the way French sentences are constructed and verbs conjugated. When you read, you learn grammar in a natural way, by simply observing and then later mimicking what you saw.

There is a problem though, depending on your level in French. Reading can be awfully slow, and therefore boring. Let's face it, you are very unlikely to keep reading in French everyday if you need to translate every word and then need five minutes to understand each sentence.

That's why it's important to choose the right text for your level. Choosing a text that is too complicated could result in you giving up. Choosing a text that is too easy means you likely won't learn anything new. What you need is a text that is easy enough to be interesting and motivating and complicated enough to be challenging. It's also important to choose a text you are interested in and not some boring school book text. You need to find a text you really want to read, something you are curious about or something funny.

If you don't know what to read, there is nothing wrong with reading a text originally written in a language other than French. Translations are often of excellent quality and only a fluent speaker and avid reader would notice a difference. Reading your favorite book in French generally works well, because you are familiar with the story and so you won't get frustrated even if you don't understand a few words.

Useful reading tools

Whatever your level is, some tools can make reading much easier. In fact, using these tools gave me the motivation to read up to ten articles per day versus one (sometimes even zero) previously.

When you start reading in French, you will often need a dictionary. The problem is that opening a dictionary every time you don't know a word takes lots of time. To save time and read faster, you can add nifty extensions to your web browser (Internet Explorer, Chrome, Firefox). With these extensions, all you have to do is click on a word to see its translation.

Google Dictionary (frenchtogether.com/go/google-dict): This Google Chrome plugin shows you the translation of any word you click on.

Lingua.ly: This great tool allows you to see the translation and hear the pronunciation of any word you click on and then save the word to review it later using a flashcard system. The app is also available on Android and IOS.

When you begin using those apps, you will stumble upon lots of unknown words, but after a few weeks, you will see that you know more and more words and reading will get easier and easier.

What to read as a beginner or intermediate learner

Let's be honest; reading when you only know a few words is tough. If you are a complete beginner, it can be wise to stick to your course's dialogues during the first weeks. Otherwise, you will spend more time translating than reading. Once you know a few hundreds words, you can start reading easy texts. This includes texts created specifically for beginners and children's stories and books. You can also find bilingual books that are written both in French and in English.

If you are interested in French news, websites like http://1jour1actu.com/ and http://www.jde.fr/ are great. These are news websites for children. While these may still be a bit complicated for complete beginners, they are a good read for intermediate learners.

You can also use http://lingq.com/, a website where you can read texts and hear the audio at the same time. You also get to select words you don't know to study later using a flashcard system. *Lingq* is an awesome app for beginners, because you can immediately see the translation of words as you read and hear the pronunciation. This means that you actually practice two core language skills at the same time: reading and listening. The website contains texts for all levels and even includes a forum where you can get help and talk with other language learners.

https://bliubliu.com/en/ works similarly. After testing your level, the website will show you movies, music clips and texts that you can partially understand. This means you won't struggle too much to understand, but you will still learn a lot.

What to read as an advanced learner?

You made it to the advanced level (congrats) and can now read more complicated and diverse texts. This includes most books and news websites.

http://www.voxeurop.eu/en and http://www.cafebabel.co.uk/ contain many articles about Europe and are available in different languages. Some articles are complicated to read, but you can easily compare the original and the translated version of each article, which makes it much easier to read.

If you are into translation, you can use the English and French version of the same article to practice.

How to make the best of a reading session

In order to reap all the benefits from a reading session, the best strategy is to save the sentences you find useful to study them later. This can be done automatically using *Lingq* or *Lingua.ly*, or you can manually choose a sentence you want to learn and copy it in a SRS software like *Anki*. When you see a useful word you didn't know, add it to your SRS. You can put the word on one side of the flashcard, and the sentence on the other side with a picture of something to help you remember it better. If the sentence is not enough for you to understand the word, add the translation.

It can be tempting to save all the new words and sentences you find in *Anki* or in another SRS software, but this can actually be counter-productive. There are words you will never read again, or words you don't really need to know at first and so learning those words would be a waste of time. You should try to be selective and only save words that seem useful or that you have read or heard a few times already.

You should also read as often as possible. By reading daily, you constantly learn new words and see words you just learned. Seeing the words you learned in another context helps you remember them better, and learning new words everyday allows you to quickly improve your understanding of French.

Chapter Ten
Listening

Why and how to listen to lots of French

Listening prepares you for real life. Reading is awesome, but at some point, you will need to listen to people and understand what they say. That's when the hours you spend listening will come in handy. By listening, you will get used to hearing the words you learn. Also, you will get used to the flow of the language and to the intonations people use when they speak French. You will even learn new words and discover different ways to use the words you already know.

Finding resources to listen to can be difficult for beginners. Even though listening to something you don't understand isn't a problem in theory because it still gives you an idea of how to pronounce words, this actually is a pretty bad idea. Why? Because listening to something you don't understand is generally frustrating and boring. As a result, you are likely to do something else at the same time and not pay much attention to what you are listening to.

Instead, I advise beginners to stick to the French course's dialogues, or to read and listen at the same time. This way you will see how to pronounce the words you learn, and will be able to understand more easily using the text. Listening and reading at the same time is can easily be done with the Kindle app or a Kindle Fire using Immersion Reading.

Once you are done listening to your course's dialogues, you can go for more advanced dialogues and resources. For example, you could use a website like *Lingq.com*, which allows you to read and listen to a text at the same time. Or you could watch French TV or watch French videos, movies and TV series with subtitles.

French Together's Youtube channel (https://www.youtube.com/user/frenchtogether) will help you find awesome French videos with subtitles.

Here are a few French TV channels you can watch online :

Euronews: You can watch programs about news, culture, technology and many other interesting topics. The language is pretty formal, but the audio of the videos is actually identical to the text written in the article under each video which makes it a very good tool to improve your understanding and see how to correctly pronounce French words. This also makes each article/video much easier to understand.

France24: This is a TV channel specifically created for people living outside of France. It gives news about France and the world and you can access it from every country.

Pluzz: This allows you to watch French public TV channels online in real time or a few hours after their broadcast. You can watch all kinds of programs, including French TV for kids, which is a great start if you are a beginner in French and don't understand more serious topics. Unfortunately, not all programs are available from abroad. You may not be able to watch everything if you are in the US or in the UK for example.

TF1: This private French TV channel also offers videos online. There is a wide variety of topics and you can easily find something corresponding to your level and taste. The videos are normally not visible from abroad; however, you can actually avoid this limitation quite easily with a VPN. You will discover how to do that below.

M6 Replay: Similar to TF1, this TV channel offers a lot of different programs. They are unfortunately not visible from outside of France without a VPN either.

Arte: This TV channel offers programs in both French and German. If you speak German, this is a great occasion to practice your French and you can easily watch the German version of the program if you didn't understand something.

RTBF: If you are interested in Belgium, you can watch this TV channel. The videos seem to be accessible without geographical restrictions.

TV5 Canada: If you are interested in Québec French, this is the right TV channel for you. You cannot watch the videos outside of Canada without a VPN though.

TV5 Monde: You can watch TV5 Monde online without VPN. This TV channel has a lot of interesting documentaries available.

A VPN is a way to tell websites you are in a country other than the one where you really are. This is extremely useful (and in some cases mandatory) to watch some French TV channels from abroad. I personally use the VPN *Hide My Ass (hidemyass.com),* because it's easy to use (you just install an app and choose your country) and fast. However, there are some other free alternatives like *Hotspotshield (hotspotshield.com)* .

Chapter Eleven
Writing

Writing is an important step in your journey...

Writing is an important step in your journey towards French mastery. In most cases, this will be the first time you actively practice French. This will be the first time you go from theory to practice.

Writing has three main goals. Getting feedback; getting used to the language; and better memorizing. When you write, you create sentences using the language you are learning and this forces you to leave your comfort zone. You no longer use English and instead, you have to get used to a new language and a new way to write. This is essential because that's when your brain really starts to get familiar with the French language. At first, writing is hard because you don't know what words to use, how to use them, and you may have to regularly open a dictionary and check conjugation tables. This is a slow, irritating process.

But just as you did for reading, speaking, and listening, you will quickly make progress with writing. Writing a sentence will soon become easy. You might even start to enjoy writing in French. Writing is good, but writing and getting feedback is better. Just as for speaking, *Italki.com* is an awesome place to start. You can post your texts there and get corrections from native speakers. These corrections often include explanations of what you did wrong. This feedback will allow you to correct your mistakes and better write and speak French. But in order to get feedback, you will need to help other people, too. The more people you help, the faster you will get corrections. You could also use *lang-8.com* for the same purpose.

If you don't have the time or desire to exchange with people on websites like *Italki* or *Lang-8*, you can use an automatic tool like http://bonpatron.com/en/. This great tool looks for common mistakes and helps you correct them. However, it can't replace feedback from a native speaker. *Bon Patron* can tell you if you didn't write a word correctly or perhaps forgot the plural, but it won't tell you if your sentence sounds weird or for some reason just doesn't make sense.

When you write, don't try to get everything perfect. You will make mistakes and that's okay. It's part of the learning process. The most important thing is to take notes so you don't make the same mistakes again. You can write about anything you want, for example, your day, a movie you watched, or describe a picture. You could even write short unrelated sentences if you are a beginner and don't feel like you can create a complete story.

Or you could talk to someone. Websites like *italki.com* and *interpals.net* are full of French people eager to improve their English. These people will be more than happy to correct your mistakes if you do the same for them in English. Having someone interesting to write to is a great motivation, too.

Chapter Twelve
Speaking

When should you speak French?

Are you terrified at the idea of speaking French? You are not alone; tens of thousands of language learners around the world feel terrified at the idea of speaking in a foreign language. You want to speak French, that's why you are learning French after all, so you have to do it. No matter how much it scares you, no matter how many excuses you invent, deep inside you, you know you will eventually need to speak French. In your mind, you can already hear all the laughs around you, see all the mocking faces surrounding you, feel the shame in your heart. You have convinced yourself that this will be the most embarrassing experience of your life.

Except this is never going to happen. Nobody is going to make fun of you. People will be happy to see you speak their language, and will often do their best to help you improve. And if someone laughs, this doesn't mean he/she is making fun of you. Most of the time, it just means that you made a funny mistake, and that's not something you should be ashamed of. Here is a list of hilarious French mistakes (frenchtogether.com/things-shouldnt-say-france). The comments are particularly interesting, because they show that mistakes are more fun than embarrassing. By speaking as soon as possible, you quickly receive feedback, which allows you to correct your mistakes, gain confidence and get used to the language.

You will also get to know French people, which can considerably boost your motivation. Having a French friend is one of the best motivation you could have. Even if all you know is how to introduce yourself in French, speaking gives you the opportunity to check if your pronunciation is correct. Otherwise, you could spend six months learning French and just assume that your pronunciation was correct when it was actually wrong. And it's much easier to change a new behavior than one that has already become a bad habit.

In addition, speaking French will keep you motivated, because once the terror of speaking French for the first time is gone, you will gain confidence and look forward to using the words and sentences you have just learned. Speaking French as soon as possible isn't only a good thing, it's a necessity.

You will discover how to find a French conversation partner in the following pages of this book.

How to find the ideal conversation partner

The fact a person speaks French doesn't mean that person would be a good conversation partner. As a beginner or intermediate learner, you need to find someone patient enough to correct you when you make mistakes and is willing to speak more slowly if you don't understand.

As a child, your parents and the people around you naturally did this for you. They made the effort to speak slowly, to repeat as necessary, and to tell you when you made mistakes. But as an adult, most people won't make this effort for you. Which means that you have two solutions, either you pay a teacher, or you find a tandem partner.

A tandem partner is a person willing to learn your language (English or any other language you speak fluently) and who will help you learn their language in return. A language partner won't cost you anything, and you will have the chance to talk to someone who accepts your mistakes and will offer you feedback to improve your French. In return, you will help your tandem partner learn English. This is an extremely fun and motivating process. You will both make progress together, help each other, and share your culture. There are lots of amazing stories of tandem partners who then became awesome friends and travelled to meet each other.

You have many solutions to find a tandem partner. If you live in a big city, you could check *Couchsurfing.org* or http://www.meetup.com/ and see if they organize weekly meetings in your city. These meetings are the perfect occasion to meet French people to practice with. You could also type "French language exchange" followed by the name of your city to see if such meetings exist in your city.

If you can't find anyone that way, don't worry! You can also find an awesome tandem partner on *italki.com*. You discovered earlier that you can use this online community to get your texts corrected, but you can also use it to find a tandem partner. Simply create an account, write a nice profile description and upload your most beautiful picture and you are good to go. Thousands of French people use *Italki* and you should be able to quickly find the perfect tandem partner for you.

If you are willing to spend money and want to work with a professional, you can also find a French teacher on *Italki*. Prices are usually very reasonable and many teachers offer trial lessons on Skype. This isn't something I tried since I prefer to meet my language partners at events like *Couchsurfing* meetings, but many French learners have successfully found a language tutor that way.

Talking to a stranger on Skype can be scary at first, but you will quickly get used to it. And if you feel you don't have anything in common with your language partner and don't enjoy the conversation, don't force yourself to keep going. You cannot get on well with everyone and it's important that you enjoy talking to your language partner. Otherwise speaking French will become something you hate doing.

When I started seriously learning English, I had a hard time finding a native English speaker to talk to. For some reason, I couldn't keep the conversation going with the language partners I found. So I ended up practicing English with non-native speakers. This wasn't ideal, of course, but I had fun and it gave me the motivation I needed to keep learning English. So if you find a non-native speaker who speaks good French and with whom you enjoy talking, keep talking to him! When it comes to learning French, the most important thing is to enjoy the process.

As a beginner, speaking to someone in French will be exhausting. You will likely feel like you can't say much, and this will frustrate you. Don't give up! You will quickly make progress and be able to create sentences and then conversations. At some point, you will realize that you have just spoken in French for 15 minutes, and it will become a pleasure.

After your first conversation in French, you will not only feel proud, you will also feel extremely motivated. Knowing you can have a conversation in French, even a basic one, will give you a reason to keep learning. This is a virtuous circle; the more you speak, the more motivated you are, and the more motivated you are, the more you want to speak.

The French-learning toolbox

Vocabulary

Memrise (memrise.com) is an awesome website where you can learn all kind of things. The website uses a Spaced Repetition System to help you memorize vocabulary. This means that the software will regularly show you words and ask if you remember their meaning. Each word will be presented to you just before you forget it. This is one of the most effective ways to learn vocabulary.

Anki (ankisrs.net) uses a SRS system like *Memrise*. But this software gives you more flexibility and you have to enter all the words and sentences by yourself.

How To Learn And Memorize The Vocabulary Of Any Language (frenchtogether.com/go.magnetic-memory) is an awesome course created by Anthony Metivier teaches you great techniques (like memory palaces) to better learn and remember vocabulary. A huge time saver.

Tatoeba (tatoeba.org) allows you to easily find example sentences.

Forvo (forvo.com) is a database of words pronounced by native speakers.

Rhinospike (rhinospike.com) If the word or sentence you are looking for isn't on Forvo, you can ask someone to pronounce it for you on Rhinospike.

Wordreference (wordreference.com) is my favorite online French dictionary. It contains lots of words and you can ask for help on the forum if you don't understand something or didn't find a definition.

Grammar

French About (french.about.com) contains lots of useful content to better understand French grammar.

The Complete & Easy French Grammar for Beginners - Level A1 (frenchtogether.com/go/french-grammar-beginner) is an online course that explains the basic concepts of French grammar and helps you get a clear understanding of how the language works. If you are confused about French grammar (who isn't), this is a great way to get started.

Bon Patron (bonpatron.com) can tell you if you made a spelling or grammar mistake.

Practice

Practice is an essential part of the learning process. These tools make it easy to find native French speakers to practice with.

Interpals (interpals.net) is the website you need if you are looking for someone to practice French with. I found many conversation partners and even made awesome friends.

Italki (italki.com) is a social network for language learners. You can use the website to practice writing and get corrected by native speakers, as well as to find private teachers and people to speak French with.

Couchsurfing (couchsurfing.org) is a community of travellers who regularly organize meetings and there is probably one near you. These meetings are great opportunities to meet French speakers and practice. I often use it to meet German speakers and it's always fun and interesting.

Meetup.com You can find lots of language exchange meetings on this website.

Lang8 (lang-8.com) is where you go if you want to get your texts corrected. You can post what you write in

French and get corrected by native French speakers. All you have to do in return is to correct other people's texts.

French courses

Assimil (assimil.com) If I had to choose a French course (I don't because I am French), I would

choose *Assimil.* This method contains high-quality dialogues, which are perfect to learn French on your own. Contrary to some other online courses, with *Assimil* you get a book you can bring with you everywhere.

Rocket French (rocketlanguages.com) teaches French using dialogues and gives you the ability to ask questions on a forum. You will also find grammar courses and games. Read the Rocket French review for more information.

Babbel (babbel.com) is similar to Rocket French. In addition to the course, you get access to a community of language learners which can be extremely motivating. Read the Babbel review for more information.

Duolingo (duolingo.com) gives you the opportunity to learn French by translating the web. It's the only free course of these selections.

Mosalingua (mosalingua.com) is an inexpensive app that's like a virtual phrasebook. It contains lots of useful sentences classified by theme and you can then review them with a SRS software included in the app. This isn't a complete French course, but can be very useful when you travel.

Last words

This book ends here, but this is not the end. *How to Learn French in a Year* is the first book I have written. It is the result of years spent learning languages and looking for the best ways to learn them in a fast and enjoyable fashion.

I hope this book helped you and provided the motivation you need to successfully learn French. If there is anything you would like to ask or suggest, feel free to contact me at benjamin@frenchtogether.com . I would be happy to help you and to know how you implemented all the advice you found in this book.

You can also go to frenchtogether.com/my-french-together to become a member of *My French Together* for free and receive weekly tips to learn French.

Yours Frenchly
Benjamin Houy

21823826R00070

Printed in Great Britain
by Amazon